How to use your Do...

MAY

Column headers (slanted): Frank | AM · Molly | PM · Ben | EVE · Anne · Don't to...

	Frank (AM)	Molly (PM)	Ben (EVE)	Anne	Don't to...
16 Monday	8.30 Give Blood / Working late	Buy seeds	Take Sims to Jamal	HUGE MATHS TEST!!	Birthday Presents for Grandad
17 Tuesday	Finish book / GOVS meeting 8pm	Tennis		Becky after school	
18 Wednesday	Dinner with Boss EL GRECO 7.30	(Key) Leaflets	BANDPRACTICE / Scout Subs {JABS}	Violin lesson 9:15am / Buy ear plugs!	Dishwasher Salt
19 Thursday		Annual Review 3pm			
20 Friday	Phoe Sean Badminton 7.00 — FINAL HOLIDAY DEPOSIT	DENTIST 4.30 ——→	Book Club Chloë's 8pm		
21 Saturday		Aromatherapy TheLab 3.00		BIN BAGS!!!	
22 Sunday	DAD'S 75th ——— Royal Oak 12.15 ——————→ Cake!				

Family use: up to 5 people—pop everyone's name at the top and their activities and appointments in the boxes underneath (or not!).

Personal use: use the boxes or write across the feint dotted lines and use the space between the slanted lines at the top to break up the day as you so wish!

THIS YEAR 2022

JANUARY
M   3 10 17 24 31
T   4 11 18 25
W   5 12 19 26
T   6 13 20 27
F   7 14 21 28
S   1 8 15 22 29
S   2 9 16 23 30

FEBRUARY
M   7 14 21 28
T   1 8 15 22
W   2 9 16 23
T   3 10 17 24
F   4 11 18 25
S   5 12 19 26
S   6 13 20 27

MARCH
M   7 14 21 28
T   1 8 15 22 29
W   2 9 16 23 30
T   3 10 17 24 31
F   4 11 18 25
S   5 12 19 26
S   6 13 20 27

APRIL
M   4 11 18 25
T   5 12 19 26
W   6 13 20 27
T   7 14 21 28
F   1 8 15 22 29
S   2 9 16 23 30
S   3 10 17 24

MAY
M   2 9 16 23 30
T   3 10 17 24 31
W   4 11 18 25
T   5 12 19 26
F   6 13 20 27
S   7 14 21 28
S   1 8 15 22 29

JUNE
M   6 13 20 27
T   7 14 21 28
W   1 8 15 22 29
T   2 9 16 23 30
F   3 10 17 24
S   4 11 18 25
S   5 12 19 26

JULY
M   4 11 18 25
T   5 12 19 26
W   6 13 20 27
T   7 14 21 28
F   1 8 15 22 29
S   2 9 16 23 30
S   3 10 17 24 31

AUGUST
M   1 8 15 22 29
T   2 9 16 23 30
W   3 10 17 24 31
T   4 11 18 25
F   5 12 19 26
S   6 13 20 27
S   7 14 21 28

SEPTEMBER
M   5 12 19 26
T   6 13 20 27
W   7 14 21 28
T   1 8 15 22 29
F   2 9 16 23 30
S   3 10 17 24
S   4 11 18 25

OCTOBER
M   3 10 17 24 31
T   4 11 18 25
W   5 12 19 26
T   6 13 20 27
F   7 14 21 28
S   1 8 15 22 29
S   2 9 16 23 30

NOVEMBER
M   7 14 21 28
T   1 8 15 22 29
W   2 9 16 23 30
T   3 10 17 24
F   4 11 18 25
S   5 12 19 26
S   6 13 20 27

DECEMBER
M   5 12 19 26
T   6 13 20 27
W   7 14 21 28
T   1 8 15 22 29
F   2 9 16 23 30
S   3 10 17 24 31
S   4 11 18 25

Key holidays & festivals for a selection of major faiths are shown in the main diary

The phases of the moon will be shown thus :-
● NEW MOON   ☽ FIRST QUARTER   ○ FULL MOON   ☾ LAST QUARTER

NEXT YEAR 2023

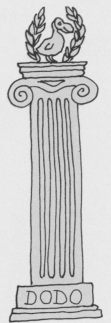

JANUARY
M   2 9 16 23 30
T   3 10 17 24 31
W   4 11 18 25
T   5 12 19 26
F   6 13 20 27
S   7 14 21 28
S   1 8 15 22 29

FEBRUARY
M   6 13 20 27
T   7 14 21 28
W   1 8 15 22
T   2 9 16 23
F   3 10 17 24
S   4 11 18 25
S   5 12 19 26

MARCH
M   6 13 20 27
T   7 14 21 28
W   1 8 15 22 29
T   2 9 16 23 30
F   3 10 17 24 31
S   4 11 18 25
S   5 12 19 26

APRIL
M   3 10 17 24
T   4 11 18 25
W   5 12 19 26
T   6 13 20 27
F   7 14 21 28
S   1 8 15 22 29
S   2 9 16 23 30

MAY
M   1 8 15 22 29
T   2 9 16 23 30
W   3 10 17 24 31
T   4 11 18 25
F   5 12 19 26
S   6 13 20 27
S   7 14 21 28

JUNE
M   5 12 19 26
T   6 13 20 27
W   7 14 21 28
T   1 8 15 22 29
F   2 9 16 23 30
S   3 10 17 24
S   4 11 18 25

JULY
M   3 10 17 24 31
T   4 11 18 25
W   5 12 19 26
T   6 13 20 27
F   7 14 21 28
S   1 8 15 22 29
S   2 9 16 23 30

AUGUST
M   7 14 21 28
T   1 8 15 22 29
W   2 9 16 23 30
T   3 10 17 24 31
F   4 11 18 25
S   5 12 19 26
S   6 13 20 27

SEPTEMBER
M   4 11 18 25
T   5 12 19 26
W   6 13 20 27
T   7 14 21 28
F   1 8 15 22 29
S   2 9 16 23 30
S   3 10 17 24

OCTOBER
M   2 9 16 23 30
T   3 10 17 24 31
W   4 11 18 25
T   5 12 19 26
F   6 13 20 27
S   7 14 21 28
S   1 8 15 22 29

NOVEMBER
M   6 13 20 27
T   7 14 21 28
W   1 8 15 22 29
T   2 9 16 23 30
F   3 10 17 24
S   4 11 18 25
S   5 12 19 26

DECEMBER
M   4 11 18 25
T   5 12 19 26
W   6 13 20 27
T   7 14 21 28
F   1 8 15 22 29
S   2 9 16 23 30
S   3 10 17 24 31

DODO   PAD

Published by Dodo Pad Ltd. PO Box 220, Tewkesbury, GL20 9FE

Compilation & Original Illustration by Naomi McBride 2021. Reprographics by Peta Bull Design.

Illustrations © Dodo Pad Ltd 2021 © B M Peak 1995, 2021 © Rose Verney 1965, 2021

Dodo Pad Desk Diary – ISBN 978 0 857702 46 3 / DodoPAX loose-leaf Diary – ISBN 978 0 87702 49 4

Printed in the UK using vegetable-based inks on sustainably sourced paper. Your Dodo Pad is 100% plastic free with a vegetable based biodegradable laminate on the cover and can be fully recycled or kept for posterity.
No Dodo Pad, that we know of, has ever been thrown away or recycled!

PERLES de SAGESSE

DOODLES

OLD CHESTNUTS

BON MOTS

THE DODO PAD

2022

This Dodo Pad is indodispensable. If found, please return to

© Rose Verney 1965, 2021 © B. M. Peak 1995, 2021

2022

JANUARY 2022

1 S	NEW YEAR'S DAY	17 M	MARTIN LUTHER KING DAY (US)
2 Su		18 T	
3 M	BANK HOLIDAY (UK, EIRE, US, AUS & NZ)	19 W	
4 T	BANK HOLIDAY (SCOT OBS)	20 Th	
5 W		21 F	
6 Th		22 S	
7 F		23 Su	
8 S		24 M	
9 Su		25 T	BURNS' NIGHT
10 M		26 W	AUSTRALIA DAY
11 T		27 Th	
12 W		28 F	
13 Th		29 S	
14 F		30 Su	
15 S		31 M	
16 Su			

FEBRUARY 2022

1 T	CHINESE NEW YEAR	17 Th	
2 W		18 F	
3 Th		19 S	
4 F		20 Su	
5 S		21 M	PRESIDENTS DAY (US)
6 Su	WAITANGI DAY (NZ)	22 T	
7 M		23 W	
8 T		24 Th	
9 W		25 F	
10 Th		26 S	
11 F		27 Su	
12 S		28 M	
13 Su			
14 M			
15 T			
16 W			

Public Holidays et al.
This information is correct at time of going to press. The publishers can accept no responsibility for any errors.

MARCH 2022

1 T	SHROVE TUESDAY	17 Th	
2 W		18 F	
3 Th		19 S	
4 F		20 Su	
5 S		21 M	
6 Su		22 T	
7 M		23 W	
8 T		24 Th	
9 W		25 F	
10 Th		26 S	
11 F		27 Su	MOTHER'S DAY (UK & EIRE) BST BEGINS
12 S		28 M	
13 Su		29 T	
14 M	CANBERRA DAY (AUS) COMMONWEALTH DAY	30 W	
15 T		31 Th	
16 W			

APRIL 2022

1 F		17 Su	EASTER DAY
2 S		18 M	EASTER MONDAY
3 Su	RAMADAN BEGINS	19 T	
4 M		20 W	
5 T		21 Th	
6 W		22 F	
7 Th		23 S	
8 F		24 Su	
9 S		25 M	ANZAC DAY (AUS & NZ)
10 Su		26 T	
11 M		27 W	
12 T		28 Th	
13 W		29 F	
14 Th		30 S	
15 F	GOOD FRIDAY		
16 S	PASSOVER		

MAY 2022

1 Su		17 T	
2 M	MAY BANK HOLIDAY (UK & EIRE)	18 W	
3 T		19 Th	
4 W		20 F	
5 Th		21 S	
6 F		22 Su	
7 S		23 M	VICTORIA DAY (CANADA)
8 Su	MOTHER'S DAY (US & AUS)	24 T	
9 M		25 W	
10 T		26 Th	
11 W		27 F	
12 Th		28 S	
13 F		29 Su	
14 S		30 M	MEMORIAL DAY (US)
15 Su		31 T	
16 M			

JUNE 2022

1 W		17 F	
2 Th	SPRING BANK HOLIDAY (UK)	18 S	
3 F	PUBLIC HOLIDAY QUEEN'S PLATINUM JUBILEE (UK)	19 Su	FATHER'S DAY (UK, US & CAN)
4 S		20 M	
5 Su		21 T	
6 M	HOLIDAY (EIRE)	22 W	
7 T		23 Th	
8 W		24 F	
9 Th		25 S	
10 F		26 Su	
11 S		27 M	
12 Su		28 T	
13 Su		29 W	
14 T		30 Th	
15 W			
16 Th			

2022

JULY 2022

1 F	CANADA DAY	17 Su	
2 s		18 M	
3 Su		19 T	
4 M	INDEPENDENCE DAY (US)	20 W	
5 T		21 Th	
6 W		22 F	
7 Th		23 s	
8 F		24 Su	
9 s		25 M	
10 Su	EID AL-ADHA	26 T	
11 M		27 W	
12 T	PUBLIC HOLIDAY (N. IRELAND)	28 Th	
13 W		29 F	
14 Th	BASTILLE DAY	30 s	ISLAMIC NEW YEAR
15 F		31 Su	
16 s			

AUGUST 2022

1 M	SUMMER BA WWNK HOLIDAY (SCOTLAND & EIRE)	17 W	
2 T		18 Th	
3 W		19 F	
4 Th		20 s	
5 F		21 Su	
6 s		22 M	
7 Su		23 T	
8 M		24 W	
9 T		25 Th	
10 W		26 F	
11 Th		27 s	
12 F		28 Su	
13 s		29 M	SUMMER BANK HOLIDAY (UK)
14 Su		30 T	
15 M		31 W	
16 T			

SEPTEMBER 2022

1 Th		17 s	
2 F		18 Su	
3 s		19 M	
4 Su	FATHER'S DAY (AUS)	20 T	
5 M	LABOR DAY (US & CAN)	21 W	
6 T		22 Th	
7 W		23 F	
8 Th		24 s	
9 F		25 Su	
10 s		26 M	ROSH HASHANAH
11 Su		27 T	
12 M		28 W	
13 T		29 Th	
14 W		30 F	
15 Th			
16 F			

OCTOBER 2022

1 s		17 M	
2 Su		18 T	
3 M		19 W	
4 T		20 Th	
5 W	YOM KIPPUR	21 F	
6 Th		22 s	
7 F		23 Su	
8 s		24 M	
9 Su		25 T	DIWALI
10 M	COLUMBUS DAY (US) THANKSGIVING (CANADA)	26 W	
11 T		27 Th	
12 W		28 F	
13 Th		29 s	
14 F		30 Su	BST ENDS
15 s		31 M	HALLOWE'EN, HOLIDAY (EIRE)
16 Su			

NOVEMBER 2022

1 T		17 Th	
2 W		18 F	
3 Th		19 s	
4 F		20 Su	
5 s	GUY FAWKES' NIGHT	21 M	
6 Su		22 T	
7 M		23 W	
8 T		24 Th	THANKSGIVING (US)
9 W		25 F	
10 Th		26 s	
11 F	VETERANS' DAY (US) REMEMBRANCE DAY (CAN)	27 Su	
12 s		28 M	
13 Su	REMEMBRANCE SUNDAY (UK)	29 T	
14 M		30 W	
15 T			
16 W			

DECEMBER 2022

1 Th		17 s	
2 F		18 Su	
3 s		19 M	HANUKKAH
4 Su		20 T	
5 M		21 W	
6 T		22 Th	
7 W		23 F	
8 Th		24 s	
9 F		25 Su	CHRISTMAS DAY
10 s		26 M	BOXING DAY (UK, AUS, NZ) ST STEPHEN'S DAY (EIRE)
11 Su		27 T	BANK HOLIDAY (UK)
12 M		28 W	
13 T		29 Th	
14 W		30 F	
15 Th		31 s	
16 F			

Where Religious Holidays are indicated, the first full day of the holiday is shown.

Lord Dodo, THE publishing baron de nos jours, was thrilled to purchase this unusual 13th Century Armenian miniature of St John the Evangelist, patron saint of publishers, with his scribe Prochorus. Proof, if it were needed, that the Dodo Pad is a revered and venerated manuscript - and has the Almighty's seal of approval!

December 2021 / January 2022

27 Monday

Bank Holiday UK   Feast of St John the Evangelist

28 Tuesday

Bank Holiday UK

29 Wednesday

30 Thursday

31 Friday

1 Saturday

New Year's Day

2 Sunday

ord Dodo was leafing through his copy of Burke's Peerage recently, when he came upon this entry for his Hibernian ancestor whose travels graced these pages some years ago. Here's an extract...

THE O'DODO OF THE CRAGS, WESTERN IRELAND

Osbert Hercules Macnamara O'Dodo, The O'Dodo, Chief of Clann na Dodo, Grand Steward of the Blaskets, President of the Crags Whiskey Appreciation Club, Patron of the O'Dodocragmore Seagull Rescue & Rehabilitation Society &, &, &

m Hon Wisteria Augusta, *dau of* Lord Headover-Heal *(pronounced 'Hevverel')* of Headover Hall, North Yorks., *and has issue.*

Clubs: Spratts, The Mackerel, Doodles, Bengal Tigers Cricket and Croquet, Les Gourmands de Strasbourg, Minette's Recreation & Cigar Divan, Barcelona, Cercle des Beaux Arts et Roulette, Biarritz.

Sons living: Hercules Macnamara, (Big Mac) *heir,* Filbert George (Nutty), Augustus Victor Macasser (Oily)

Daughters living: Wisteria Desirée. Aloe Vera Agapantha, Semolina Auricula, Amnesia Sequoia

Collateral branch of the present Lord Dodo (*qv*). Established in Western Ireland under the patronage of Queen Elizabeth I, from whom they received hereditary titles, rights and privileges.

January 2022

3 Monday

New Year's Day (obs) UK, IRE, US, AUS, NZ

4 Tuesday

New Year's Bank Holiday SCOT

5 Wednesday

1786 Birth of John Bernard Burke, genealogist, who assisted his father in producing the first edition of Burke's Peerage

6 Thursday

7 Friday

8 Saturday

9 Sunday

Sam Spade, Mr Hammett's hard—boiled
detective hero, was used to receiving threats
and cryptic notes, working as he did on the
seedier side of the tracks. However this
anonymous letter not only tested his detecting
skills, but also his lingual dexterity. Try
reading it out loud—quickly!

SWIM SAM SWIM
SHOVE THEM
YOU'RE A SWIMMER
SIX HARP
SHARKS SEEK
SMALL SNACKS
SO SWIM
SAM SWIM

JANUARY 2022

10 MONDAY

1961 Death of Dashiell Hammett, author of 'The Maltese Falcon'

11 TUESDAY

12 WEDNESDAY

13 THURSDAY

14 FRIDAY

15 SATURDAY

16 SUNDAY

Lord Dodo has always been an avid collector of rare and unusual books, but this one really took the biscuit...

I finally procured this first edition of Roget's Thesaurus. When I opened it, all the pages were blank. There are no words to describe how angry I am.

JANUARY
2022

Week 3

17
Monday

Martin Luther King Day US   O

18
Tuesday

1779   Birth of Peter Mark Roget

19
Wednesday

20
Thursday

21
Friday

22
Saturday

23
Sunday

January
2022

24 Monday

25 Tuesday
Burns Night

26 Wednesday
Australia Day

27 Thursday

28 Friday

29 Saturday

30 Sunday

Week 4

1905 Discovery of the Cullinan diamond, the largest diamond ever found, in a South African mine

What's the best thing about Switzerland?

Well, they may have been way behind the times in giving women the vote, but their flag is a huge plus.

JF 2022

January February

31 Monday

1 Tuesday

2 Wednesday

3 Thursday

4 Friday

5 Saturday

6 Sunday

Week 5

Chinese New Year   1959   First Swiss referendum on women's suffrage

Waitangi Day NZ

I would like to make a pun about philosophy, but I Kant.

Gimlet-eyed Dodopadlers will see that, for this obscure sequel to his masterwork, the Critique of Pure Reason, Herr Kant was obliged to enlist the help of fellow thinker, Lord Dodo.

FEBRUARY 2022

7 Monday

8 Tuesday

9 Wednesday

10 Thursday

11 Friday

12 Saturday

13 Sunday

Week 6

1804 Death of philosopher Immanuel Kant

I'm a funghi to be with

BE MY VALENTINE

FEBRUARY
2022

Week 7

14 Monday

Valentines Day

15 Tuesday

16 Wednesday

○

17 Thursday

18 Friday

19 Saturday

20 Sunday

oor Lord Dodo! Once again
he was on his way to the printers
with his Lexicon for the 21st Century
when some new entries arrived
that he felt merited inclusion.
Back to the drawing board...

adamant–the first male ant
torture–like a torch, only more so
minion–a tiny shallot
falsetto–fake ice cream cone
macaroon–a Scotsman on a desert island
fielding–to find a bell in the dark
diagnose–a proboscis which starts on
the top left of the face and finishes on
the bottom right

February

2022

21 Monday

Presidents' Day US

22 Tuesday

23 Wednesday

24 Thursday

25 Friday

26 Saturday

27 Sunday

22 February 1816 Publication of John Pickering's 'A Vocabulary or Collection of Words & Phrases which have been supposed to be peculiar to the United States'

How do you know
when a bison's about to
charge?

He gets out his
credit card

February-March 2022

Week 9

28 Monday

1 Tuesday
St David's Day   Shrove Tuesday

2 Wednesday
Ash Wednesday   ●

3 Thursday

4 Friday

5 Saturday

6 Sunday

1 March 1872   Yellowstone became the world's first National Park; containing the largest herd of wild bison in the US

FRAUEN-TAG
8. MÄRZ 2022

March 2022

7 Monday

8 Tuesday

9 Wednesday

10 Thursday

11 Friday

12 Saturday

13 Sunday

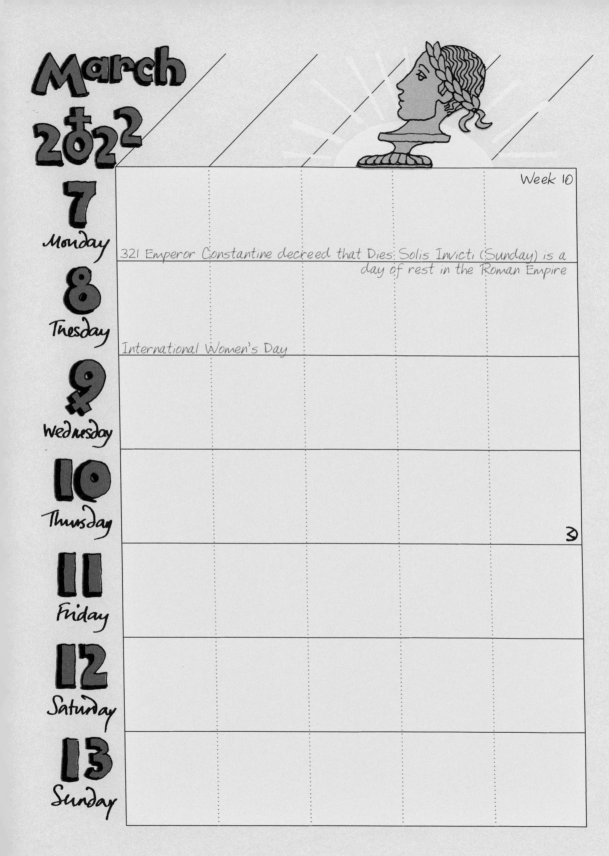

Week 10

321 Emperor Constantine decreed that Dies Solis Invicti (Sunday) is a day of rest in the Roman Empire

International Women's Day

3

What do you call a labrador that can do magic tricks?

A Labracadabrador

MARCH
2022

14
Monday

Week 11

Canberra Day AUS   Commonwealth Day   DST begins US

15
Tuesday

16
Wednesday

17
Thursday

St Patrick's Day IRE

18
Friday

○

19
Saturday

1921 Birth of magician & comedian Tommy Cooper

20
Sunday

Spring Equinox

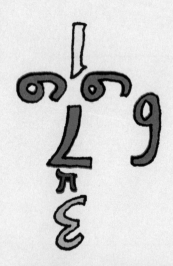

ALTERNATIVE FACT

Mr Erdos, a mathematical colossus of the 20th century, was very eccentric indeed. Apparently he was so fearful of negative numbers that he would stop at nothing to avoid them.

MARCH
2022

21 Monday

22 Tuesday

23 Wednesday

24 Thursday

25 Friday

26 Saturday

1913 Birth of Paul Erdos, renowned Hungarian mathematician

BST begins

27 Sunday

Mother's Day UK & IRE

28
Monday

29
Tuesday

Holi   1848 Niagara Falls freezes over because of an ice jam

30
Wednesday

31
Thursday

1
Friday

●

2
Saturday

DST ends AUS & NZ

3
Sunday

Ramadan begins

Week 13

St Patrick driving the snakes
out of Ireland

APRIL
2022

4 Monday

5 Tuesday

6 Wednesday

7 Thursday

8 Friday

9 Saturday

10 Sunday

Week 14

432 St Patrick returned to Ireland as a missionary bishop

A flea and a fly in a flue
were imprisoned so what could they do?
Said the flea "let us fly"
said the fly" let us flee"
so they flew through a flaw in the flue.

APRIL 2022

11 Monday

12 Tuesday

13 Wednesday

14 Thursday
Baisakhi

15 Friday
Good Friday

16 Saturday
Passover   ○

17 Sunday
Easter Sunday   1899 Birth of entomologist Vincent Wigglesworth

More Dodubious Information

St Felix of Dunwich founded a boys' school in the area around 631 AD. He immediately took the junior class bathing in the somewhat uninviting-looking North Sea. 'I'll test the water first', he reportedly said, and the place became known thereafter as Felix's Toe.

april
2022

Week 16

18 Monday

Easter Monday

19 Tuesday

20 Wednesday

21 Thursday

22 Friday

23 Saturday

St George's Day   Feast Day of St Felix the Martyr

24 Sunday

An Oxford comma walks into a bar, where it spends the evening watching the television, drinking, and smoking cigars.

• An oxymoron walked into a bar, and the silence was deafening.

• A malapropism walks into a bar, looking for all intensive purposes like a wolf in cheap clothing, muttering epitaphs and casting dispersions on his magnificent other, who takes him for granite.

• A non sequitur walks into a bar. In a strong wind, even turkeys can fly.

• Papyrus and Comic Sans walk into a bar. The barman says, "Get out–we don't serve your type."

• A mixed metaphor walks into a bar, sees the writing on the wall but hopes to nip it in the bud.

• At the end of the day, a cliché walks into a bar– fresh as a daisy, cute as a button, and sharp as a tack.

• The past, present, and future walked into a bar. It was tense.

• A dyslexic walks into a bra.

• A verb walks into a bar, sees a beautiful noun, and suggests they conjugate. The noun declines.

Jill Thomas Doyle

APRIL
MAY
2022

Week 17

25
MONDAY
ANZAC Day

26
TUESDAY

27
WEDNESDAY

28
THURSDAY

29
FRIDAY

30
SATURDAY
1912 Death of Henry Sweet, grammarian, philologist & phoneticist

SUNDAY

ALTERNATIVE FACT

Meet Anya, Karl Marx's less well-known younger sister, Anya's claim to fame was the invention of the starting pistol...

MAY 2022

2 Monday

May Bank Holiday UK & IRE

3 Tuesday

Eid al-Fitr

4 Wednesday

5 Thursday

1818 Birth of Karl Marx

6 Friday

7 Saturday

8 Sunday

Mother's Day US & AUS

More
Dodubious Information

It was a visit to Lord Dodo's highland seat for a grouse-shooting weekend many years ago that provided Walt with the inspiration for the fairytale castle in Disneyland. As a thank you, he dispatched Mickey and Minnie over to Scotland to make a surprise appearance at Little Lady Verucca Dodo's 8th birthday party. Imagine her delight!

May 2022

9 Monday

10 Tuesday

11 Wednesday

12 Thursday

13 Friday

14 Saturday

15 Sunday

Week 19

Visakha Puja Day   1928 Mickey Mouse made his first ever appearance
in the silent film 'Plane Crazy'

PROOF, IF PROOF WERE NEEDED, THAT THE DODO PAD IS ETERNALLY INDODISPENSABLE

MAY 2022

6 Monday

7 Tuesday

8 Wednesday

9 Thursday

20 Friday

21 Saturday

22 Sunday

2018 Death of Zhao Kangmin, Chinese archaeologist who discovered the Terracotta Army

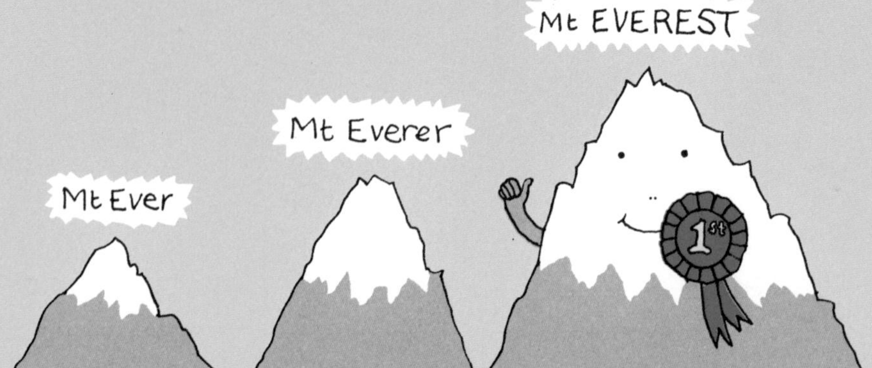
Mt Ever
Mt Everer
Mt EVEREST
1st

MAY 2022

23 MONDAY

Victoria Day CAN

24 TUESDAY

25 WEDNESDAY

26 THURSDAY

27 FRIDAY

28 SATURDAY

29 SUNDAY

Week 21

1953 First ascent of Mt Everest by Edmund Hillary and Sherpa Tensing

What sort of cheese
would you use to hide
a horse?

MASCARPONE

What does cheese say when
it looks in the mirror?

HALLOUMI

What cheese can you use to tempt a bear?

CAMEMBERT

may —
June
2022

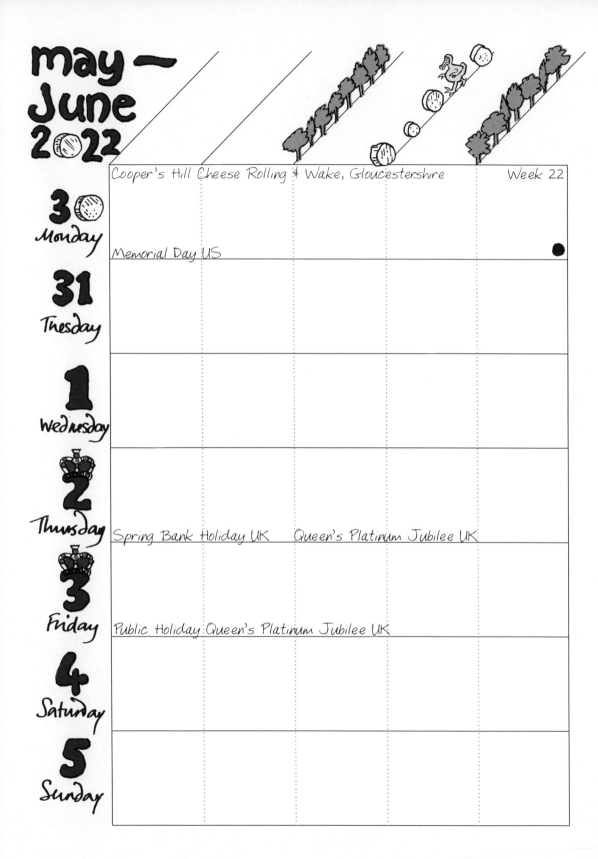

Cooper's Hill Cheese Rolling & Wake, Gloucestershire   Week 22

30 Monday

Memorial Day US

31 Tuesday

1 Wednesday

2 Thursday

Spring Bank Holiday UK   Queen's Platinum Jubilee UK

3 Friday

Public Holiday Queen's Platinum Jubilee UK

4 Saturday

5 Sunday

June 2022

6 MONDAY

7 TUESDAY

8 WEDNESDAY

9 THURSDAY

10 FRIDAY

11 SATURDAY

12 SUNDAY

Bank Holiday IRE   Queen's Birthday NZ

3

1922 First showing of 'Nanook of the North', pioneering documentary about the Inuits of northern Canada

Does the Magna Carta mean nothing to you? Did she die in vain?

Tony Hancock in 'Hancock's Half Hour'
written by Galton & Simpson

June
2022

13
Monday

Queen's Birthday AUS

14
Tuesday

○

15
Wednesday

1215 King John signed the Magna Carta

16
Thursday

17
Friday

18
Saturday

19
Sunday

Father's Day UK US & CAN

Unexpected item in the
BAGGINS area

JUNE
2022

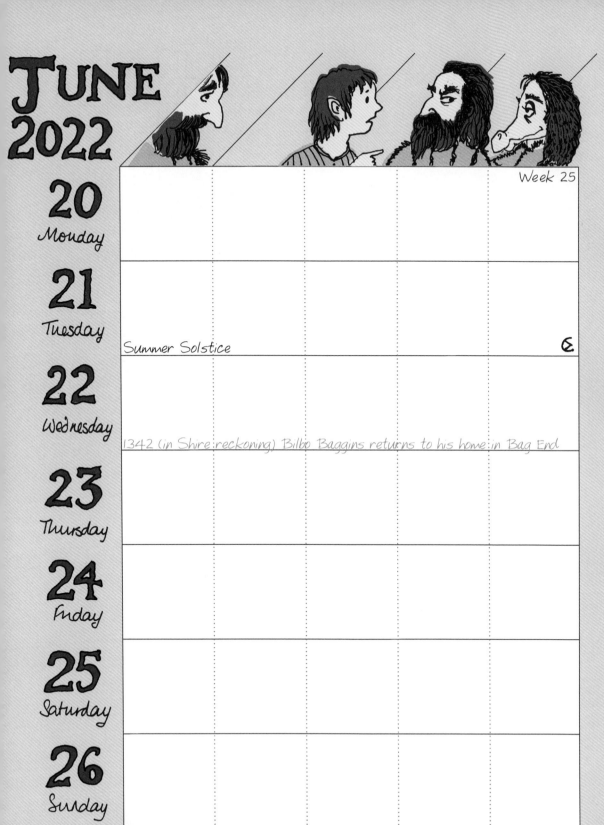

Week 25

20 Monday

21 Tuesday

Summer Solstice

22 Wednesday

1342 (in Shire reckoning) Bilbo Baggins returns to his home in Bag End

23 Thursday

24 Friday

25 Saturday

26 Sunday

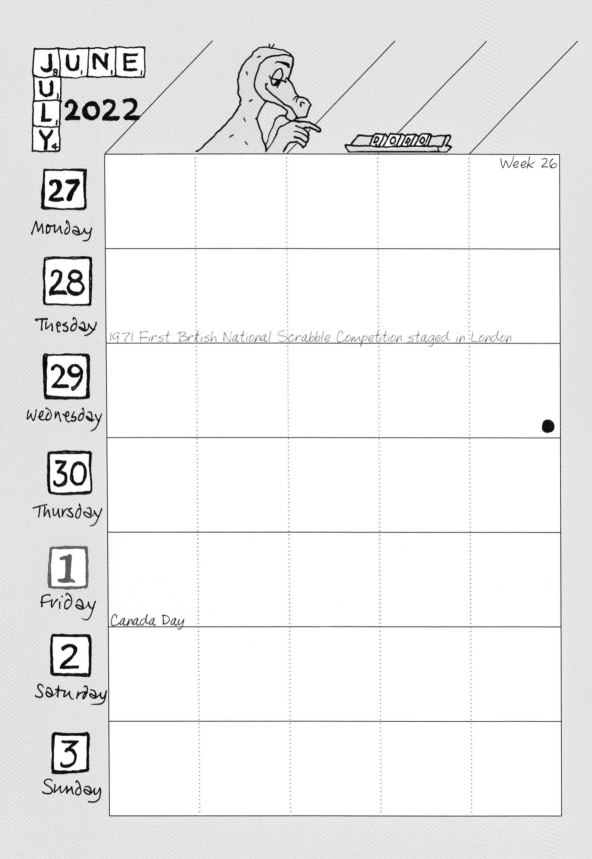

JUNE 2022

JULY

27 Monday

28 Tuesday

1971 First British National Scrabble Competition staged in London

29 Wednesday

30 Thursday

1 Friday

Canada Day

2 Saturday

3 Sunday

The Buddhist monk who saw
the face of Jesus in his margarine

Week 27

4 Monday

Independence Day US

5 Tuesday

6 Wednesday

1935 Birth of Dalai Lama

7 Thursday

8 Friday

9 Saturday

10 Sunday

Eid al-Adha

Lord Dodo's UK sales team are never daunted by the weather. The arrival of the new Dodo Pad always attracts a crowd, rain, hail or shine.

July 2022

11 Monday

12 Tuesday
Holiday NI

13 Wednesday
Obon ○

14 Thursday
Bastille Day

15 Friday
St Swithin's Day

16 Saturday

17 Sunday

What's this? Another pyramid has popped up along the banks of the Nile! Can you draw the new pyramid using one continuous line - without the line crossing itself or going back over any part already drawn? Solution in the Appendix.

July
2022

18 Monday

19 Tuesday

20 Wednesday

21 Thursday

22 Friday

23 Saturday

24 Sunday

1970 Aswan High Dam opened in Egypt, enabling human control of Nile flooding

Asalha Puja Day

 *DoDo*

Sir, Saturday morning, though recurring at regular and well-foreseen intervals, always seems to take this railway by surprise. WS Gilbert - a letter to the station-master at Baker St, on the Metropolitan Line.

JULY 2022

TRAINS | **WAY OUT**

Week 30

25 Monday

1814 George Stephenson introduced his first steam locomotive

26 Tuesday

27 Wednesday

28 Thursday

29 Friday

30 Saturday

Islamic New Year

31 Sunday

After a root and branch overhaul of the Dodocorp marketing strategy, His Lordship enlisted some local expertise in the shires, who led the sales team over hill and dale and even into the deepest forests, to ensure 100% Dodo coverage countrywide.

AUGUST 2022

1 Monday

Summer Bank Holiday SCOT & IRE

2 Tuesday

3 Wednesday

4 Thursday

5 Friday

6 Saturday

7 Sunday

1964 Prometheus, at approx. 4862 years old the world's oldest tree, was accidentally cut down in Nevada, US

Lady Dodo is a bit old-fashioned about swimwear, and hates to see her daughters in today's tiny bikinis, concurring with Modern Girl magazine of 1957: "It is hardly necessary to waste words over the so-called bikini since it is inconceivable that any girl with tact and decency would ever wear such a thing." Her loathing stems from a traumatic incident many years ago, when she was apprehended by the Swimsuit Police for the brevity of her outfit while on a family holiday in the USA. A very public humiliation that has scarred her for life...

AUGUST 2024

8 Monday

1960   The single 'Itsy Bitsy Teenie Weenie Yellow Polka Dot Bikini' hit No 1

9 Tuesday

10 Wednesday

11 Thursday

02 Friday   ○

03 Saturday

04 Sunday

WHEAT INTOLERANCE

August 2022

15 Monday

16 Tuesday

17 Wednesday

18 Thursday

19 Friday

20 Saturday

21 Sunday

Krishna Janmashtami

1865 Birth of HV Makay, inventor of the first commercially viable combine harvester

DODECLINE AND FALL

PUELLA RIGENSIS RIDEBAT
QUAM TIGRIS IN TERGO
VEHEBAT
EXTERNA PROFECTA
INTERNA REVECTA
RISUSQUE CUM TIGRE
MANEBAT

Lord Dodo has unearthed this rare example of a Roman limerick for you to translate. Answer in the Appendix (and a hint in the illustrations opposite!)

August 2022

Week 34

22 Monday

23 Tuesday

24 Wednesday
79 Death of Pliny the Elder

25 Thursday

26 Friday

27 Saturday

28 Sunday

Beatrix Potter insisted that her characters were as well-organised as she was, so she supplied them all with Dodo Pads each year, hot off the press.

Week 35

29 Monday

Summer Bank Holiday UK

30 Tuesday

31 Wednesday

1 Thursday

2 Friday

3 Saturday

4 Sunday

Father's Day AUS   1893 Beatrix Potter first wrote 'Peter Rabbit'

BAD CHAMELEON KARMA

September 2022

5 Monday

Labor Day US & CAN 1983 Release of Culture Club's 'Karma Chameleon'

6 Tuesday

7 Wednesday

8 Thursday

9 Friday

10 Saturday

○

11 Sunday

September 2022

12 Monday

13 Tuesday

14 Wednesday

15 Thursday

16 Friday

17 Saturday

18 Sunday

1940 Four boys followed their dog down a hole in Lascaux, France, and discovered extensive 17,000 year old cave paintings

19 Monday

20 Tuesday

21 Wednesday

22 Thursday

23 Friday

Autumn Equinox

24 Saturday

DST begins NZ

25 Sunday

●

ESPIONAGE

And what do you do?

I'm a spy, ma'am.

Then why are you dressed as a shepherd?

Because I'm a shepherd spy, ma'am.

Rosh Hashanah

Week 39

26 Monday

1907 Birth of Anthony Blunt, Keeper of the Queen's Pictures, later
unmasked as a Soviet agent

27 Tuesday

28 Wednesday

29 Thursday

30 Friday

1 Saturday

2 Sunday

DST begins AUS

This is my stepladder.

I never knew my real ladder.

OCTOBER 2022

3 MONDAY

4 TUESDAY

5 WEDNESDAY

6 THURSDAY

7 FRIDAY

8 SATURDAY

9 SUNDAY

Week 40

Labour Day AUS   3

Dasara

Yom Kippur

1999 DIY SOS was first broadcast on BBC

O

'Ending a sentence with a preposition is nothing to be afraid of'

Anon

OCTOBER 2022

10 Monday

Columbus Day US   Thanksgiving CAN

11 Tuesday

12 Wednesday

13 Thursday

14 Friday

15 Saturday

16 Sunday

1758 Birth of Noah Webster, grammarian & lexicographer

THE CURE FOR ANYTHING IS SALT WATER - SWEAT, TEARS OR THE SEA
ISAK DINESEN

October
2022

17
Monday

ɛ

18
Tuesday

1961 Matisse's 'Le Bateau' was hung upside down in the Museum of Modern Art, NYC, and remained thus unnoticed for 2 months

19
Wednesday

20
Thursday

21
Friday

22
Saturday

23
Sunday

Can any gimlet-eyed Dodopadlers spot the deliberate mistake in the drawing of Matisse above? Answer in the Appendix...

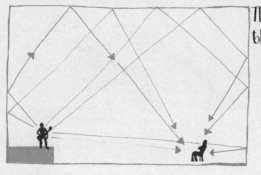

The sound from a musician on stage bounces off the auditrium walls to surround the audience...

...the sound from a pigeon on stage does not do this because - a coo sticks

COO

October
2022

24 Monday

Labour Day NZ

25 Tuesday

Diwali

26 Wednesday

27 Thursday

28 Friday

29 Saturday

30 Sunday

1783 Death of Jean-Baptiste le Rond d'Alembert, early pioneer of acoustics

BST ends

What is this that roareth thus?
Can it be a Motor Bus?
Yes, the smell and hideous hum
Indicat Motorem Bum!...
How shall wretches live like us
Cincti Bis Motoribus?
Domine, defende nos
Contra hos Motores Bos!

A D Godley

OCTOBER
NOVEMBER
2022

31 Monday

Halloween   Holiday ROI

1 Tuesday

Melbourne Cup Day AUS   1915 Mrs G Duncan became the first female bus driver in London

2 Wednesday

3 Thursday

4 Friday

5 Saturday

Guy Fawkes' Night

6 Sunday

DST ends US

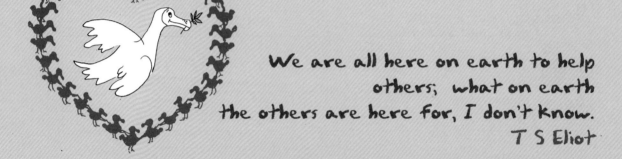

We are all here on earth to help
others; what on earth
the others are here for, I don't know.
T S Eliot

NOVEMBER 2022

Week 45

7 Monday

Guru Nanak's Birthday

8 Tuesday

○

9 Wednesday

10 Thursday

11 Friday

Veterans Day US   Remembrance Day CAN

12 Saturday

13 Sunday

Remembrance Sunday UK   World Kindness Day

Astronomers got fed up watching the moon going round the earth for 24 hours....

....so they decided to call it a day

november
2022

14 Monday

1971 Mariner 9, an unmanned space probe, began to orbt Mars

15 Tuesday

16 Wednesday

17 Thursday

18 Friday

19 Saturday

20 Sunday

SELFISH FRENCH COWS

NOVEMBER 2022

21 Monday

22 Tuesday

23 Wednesday

●

24 Thursday

Thanksgiving US

25 Friday

1884 First patent of evaporated milk by John B Meyenberg

26 Saturday

27 Sunday

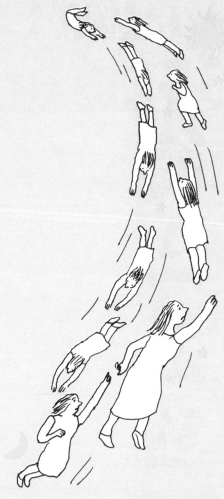

There was a young lady called Bright
Who travelled much faster than light
She departed one day
In a relative way
And came back on the previous night
Anon

November
December
2022

28 Monday

29 Tuesday

30 Wednesday

1 Thursday

2 Friday

3 Saturday

4 Sunday

1919 Einstein's Essay 'Time, Space & Gravitation' was first published

St Andrew's Day

To: Renovating heaven and adjusting the stars, washing the servant of the high Priest and putting carmine on his cheeks, and brightening up the flames of hell, putting a new tail on the Devil, and doing odd jobs for the damned, and correcting the Ten Commandments.

from a post-Reformation decorator's bill for work on a 'Doom' painting in Telscombe Church, Sussex

December
2022

5 Monday

6 Tuesday

7 Wednesday

8 Thursday

9 Friday

10 Saturday

11 Sunday

Week 49

○

1999 Unveiling of the final stage of the restoration of Michelangelo's
Last Judgment fresco in the Sistine Chapel, by Pope John Paul II

December 2022

⚓ **2** Monday

⚓ **3** Tuesday

⚓ **4** Wednesday

⚓ **5** Thursday

⚓ **6** Friday

⚓ **7** Saturday

1907 Death of eminent physicist Lord Kelvin, who was also instrumental in the design and development of the first transatlantic cable

⚓ **8** Sunday

Jesus was born at Christmas morn in a manger fild with stor Phaps it sonwd withowd a sound as wise mens gifts lay on the grownd I wunder if the as and carf where intrestid for a start it ses away in a manger no noys at all but the as and carf must have ben very sprysed wen they saw there eting and drincing trof full of baybey Jesus King of all  Kings so it must of ben allermig seeing the animall going iyor and looking very crosly at Jesus in the trof of cors Jesus was cumfy and the animalls where not becos they wantid to get there food but of cors they just had to poot up with it didnt they.

Sent to Lord Dodo by Crispian Brown, aged 6, in 1978 Where is he now?

December 2022

19 Monday

Hanukkah

20 Tuesday

21 Wednesday

Winter Solstice

22 Thursday

23 Friday

24 Saturday

25 Sunday

Christmas Day

The thing is not a nose at all but a bit
of primordial chaos slapped upon my face
H G Wells

December 2022 January 2023

Week 52

26 Monday
Boxing Day UK, AUS NZ   St Stephen's Day IRE

27 Tuesday
Bank Holiday UK   1897 First performance of 'Cyrano de Bergerac'

28 Wednesday

29 Thursday

30 Friday

31 Saturday

1 Sunday
New Year's Day

Lord Dodo is very fond, indeed a little too fond, of the festive food and revelry that accompanies Christmas at Dodo Towers, and the dawning of the New Year always causes him to reflect ruefully on these words of Edna St Vincent Millay...

My candle burns at both ends;
It will not last the night;
But ah, my foes, and oh, my friends –
It gives a lovely light!

January 2023

Week 1

2 Monday

New Year's Holiday UK, IRE, US, AUS, NZ

3 Tuesday

Holiday SCOT

4 Wednesday

5 Thursday

6 Friday

○

7 Saturday

8 Sunday

JANUARY 2023

FEBRUARY 2023

MARCH 2023

APRIL 2023

MAY 2023

JUNE 2023

FORWARD PLANNER 2023

JANUARY 2023

1 Su	NEW YEAR'S DAY (UK, EIRE, U.S, AUS & NZ)		17 T		
2 M	BANK HOLIDAY (UK)		18 W		
3 T	BANK HOLIDAY (SCOT)		19 Th		
4 W			20 F		
5 Th			21 S		
6 F			22 Su	CHINESE NEW YEAR.	
7 S			23 M		
8 Su			24 T		
9 M			25 W	BURNS' NIGHT	
10 T			26 Th	AUSTRALIA DAY	
11 W			27 F		
12 Th			28 S		
13 F			29 Su		
14 S			30 M		
15 Su			31 T		
16 M	MARTIN LUTHER KING DAY (US)				

FEBRUARY 2023

1 W		17 F		
2 Th		18 S		
3 F		19 Su		
4 S		20 M	PRESIDENTS' DAY (US)	
5 Su		21 T	SHROVE TUESDAY	
6 M	WAITANGI DAY (NZ)	22 W		
7 T		23 Th		
8 W		24 F		
9 Th		25 S		
10 F		26 Su		
11 S		27 M		
12 Su		28 T		
13 M				
14 T				
15 W				
16 Th				

Public Holidays et al.
This information is correct at time of going to press. The publishers can accept no responsibility for any errors.

MARCH 2023

1 W		17 F		
2 Th		18 S		
3 F		19 Su	MOTHER'S DAY (UK & EIRE)	
4 S		20 M		
5 Su		21 T		
6 M		22 W	RAMADAN BEGINS	
7 T		23 Th		
8 W		24 F		
9 Th		25 S		
10 F		26 Su	BST BEGINS	
11 S		27 M		
12 Su		28 T		
13 M	CANBERRA DAY (AUS) COMMONWEALTH DAY	29 W		
14 T		30 Th		
15 W		31 F		
16 Th				

APRIL 2023

1 S		17 M		
2 Su		18 T		
3 M		19 W		
4 T		20 Th		
5 W	PASSOVER	21 F		
6 Th		22 S		
7 F	GOOD FRIDAY	23 Su		
8 S		24 M		
9 Su	EASTER DAY	25 T	ANZAC DAY (AUS & NZ)	
10 M	EASTER MONDAY	26 W		
11 T		27 Th		
12 W		28 F		
13 Th		29 S		
14 F		30 Su		
15 S				
16 Su				

MAY 2023

1 M	MAY BANK HOLIDAY (UK & EIRE)	17 W		
2 T		18 Th		
3 W		19 F		
4 Th		20 S		
5 F		21 Su		
6 S		22 M	VICTORIA DAY (CANADA)	
7 Su		23 T		
8 M		24 W		
9 T		25 Th		
10 W		26 F		
11 Th		27 S		
12 F		28 Su		
13 S		29 M	MEMORIAL DAY (US) SPRING BANK HOLIDAY (UK)	
14 Su	MOTHER'S DAY (US & AUS)	30 T		
15 M		31 W		
16 T				

JUNE 2023

1 Th		17 S		
2 F		18 Su	FATHER'S DAY (UK, US & CAN)	
3 S		19 M		
4 Su		20 T		
5 M	BANK HOLIDAY (EIRE)	21 W		
6 T		22 Th		
7 W		23 F		
8 Th		24 S		
9 F		25 Su		
10 S		26 M		
11 Su		27 T		
12 M		28 W		
13 T		29 Th	EID AL-ADHA	
14 W		30 F		
15 Th				
16 F				

FORWARD PLANNER 2023

JULY 2023

1 S	CANADA DAY	17 M	
2 Su		18 T	
3 M		19 W	ISLAMIC NEW YEAR
4 T	INDEPENDENCE DAY (US)	20 Th	
5 W		21 F	
6 Th		22 S	
7 F		23 Su	
8 S		24 M	
9 Su		25 T	
10 M		26 W	
11 T		27 Th	
12 W	PUBLIC HOLIDAY (N. IRELAND)	28 F	
13 Th		29 S	
14 F	BASTILLE DAY	30 Su	
15 S		31 M	
16 Su			

AUGUST 2023

1 T		17 Th	
2 W		18 F	
3 Th		19 S	
4 F		20 Su	
5 S		21 M	
6 Su		22 T	
7 M	SUMMER BANK HOLIDAY (SCOTLAND & EIRE)	23 W	
8 T		24 Th	
9 W		25 F	
10 Th		26 S	
11 F		27 Su	
12 S		28 M	SUMMER BANK HOLIDAY (UK)
13 Su		29 T	
14 M		30 W	
15 T		31 Th	
16 W			

SEPTEMBER 2023

1 F		17 Su	
2 S		18 M	
3 Su	FATHER'S DAY (AUS)	19 T	
4 M	LABOR DAY (US & CAN)	20 W	
5 T		21 Th	
6 W		22 F	
7 Th		23 S	
8 F		24 Su	
9 S		25 M	YOM KIPPUR
10 Su		26 T	
11 M		27 W	
12 T		28 Th	
13 W		29 F	
14 Th		30 S	
15 F			
16 S	ROSH HASHANAH		

OCTOBER 2023

1 Su		17 T	
2 M		18 W	
3 T		19 Th	
4 W		20 F	
5 Th		21 S	
6 F		22 Su	
7 S		23 M	
8 Su		24 T	
9 M	COLUMBUS DAY (US) THANKSGIVING (CANADA)	25 W	
10 T		26 Th	
11 W		27 F	
12 Th		28 S	
13 F		29 Su	BST ENDS
14 S		30 M	HOLIDAY (EIRE)
15 Su		31 T	HALLOWE'EN
16 M			

NOVEMBER 2023

1 W		17 F	
2 Th		18 S	
3 F		19 Su	
4 S		20 M	
5 Su	GUY FAWKES' NIGHT	21 T	
6 M		22 W	
7 T		23 Th	THANKSGIVING (US)
8 W		24 F	
9 Th		25 S	
10 F		26 Su	
11 S	VETERANS' DAY (US) REMEMBRANCE DAY (CAN)	27 M	
12 Su	REMEMBRANCE SUNDAY (UK) DIWALI	28 T	
13 M		29 W	
14 T		30 Th	
15 W			
16 Th			

DECEMBER 2023

1 F		17 Su	
2 S		18 M	
3 Su		19 T	
4 M		20 W	
5 T		21 Th	
6 W		22 F	
7 Th		23 S	
8 F	HANUKKAH	24 Su	
9 S		25 M	CHRISTMAS DAY
10 Su		26 T	BOXING DAY (UK, AUS, NZ) ST.STEPHEN'S DAY (EIRE)
11 M		27 W	
12 T		28 Th	
13 W		29 F	
14 Th		30 S	
15 F		31 Su	
16 S			

Where Religious Holidays are indicated, the first full day of the holiday is shown.

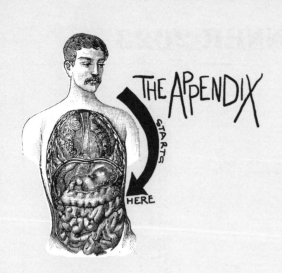

THE APPENDIX

STARTS

HERE

Solution to pyramid puzzle opposite 18th July

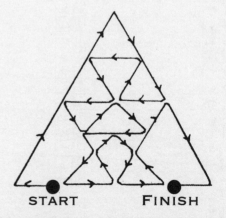

START   FINISH

APPENDIX

Translation of limerick opposite 24th August :-
There was a young lady from Riga
Who went for a ride on a tiger
They returned from the ride
With the lady inside
And a smile on the face of the tiger

APPENDIX

Dodeliberate mistake in week commencing 17th October

Matisse's 'Le Bateau' was not an oil painting, but one of his famous 'paper-cuts' using cut and coloured paper, a technique he employed to great effect in his old age, as his eyesight failed him